The Quotation Bank for A-Level

King Lear

William Shakespeare

Copyright © 2023 Esse Publishing Limited and Patrick Cragg
The moral rights of the authors have been asserted.

First published in 2023 by:
The Quotation Bank
Esse Publishing Limited
10 9 8 7 6 5 4 3 2 1

A CIP catalogue record for this book is available from the British Library.
ISBN 978-1-7396080-2-6

All enquiries to: contact@thequotationbank.co.uk
Every effort has been made to trace and contact all relevant copyright holders. However, if contacted the publisher will rectify any omission or error at the earliest opportunity.

Printed and bound by Target Print Limited, Broad Lane, Cottenham, Cambridge CB24 8SW.

www.thequotationbank.co.uk

Introduction

Quotations

Revision and Essay Planning

Welcome to The Quotation Bank, the comprehensive guide to all the key quotations you need to succeed in your exams.

Whilst you may have read the play, watched a film adaptation, understood the plot and have a strong grasp of context, all questions in your A-Levels require you to write a focused essay, full of textual references and quotations (be they textual, critical or contextual), and most importantly, quotations that you then analyse.

I think we all agree it is **analysis** that is the tricky part – and that is why we are here to help!

The Quotation Bank takes 25 of the most important quotations from the text, interprets them, analyses them, highlights literary techniques Shakespeare has used, puts them in context, and suggests which quotations you might use in which essays. We have also included 10 contextual and critical quotations, analysed them, and linked them closely to the text, all for you to explore.

At the end of **The Quotation Bank** we have put together a performance history and great revision exercises to help you prepare for your exam. We have also included a detailed glossary to make sure you completely understand what certain literary terms actually mean!

How The Quotation Bank can help you in your exams.

The Quotation Bank is designed to make sure every point you make in an essay clearly fulfils the Assessment Objectives an examiner will be using when marking your work.

Every quotation comes with the following detailed material:

Interpretation: The interpretation of each quotation allows you to fulfil **AO1**, articulating an informed, personal response, and **AO5**, using different interpretations to inform your exploration of the text.

Techniques: Using associated concepts and terminology (in this case, the techniques used by Shakespeare) is a key part of **AO1**, and can help you identify and analyse ways in which meanings are shaped (**AO2**).

Analysis: We have provided as much analysis (**AO2**) as possible, as well as exploring the significance and influence of contextual material (**AO3**) and different interpretations (**AO5**). It is a great idea to analyse the quotation in detail – you need to do more than just say what it means, but also try to explore a variety of different ways of interpreting it.

Use in essays on… Your answer needs to be focused to fulfil **AO1**. This section helps you choose relevant quotations and link them together for a stronger, more detailed essay.

How to use The Quotation Bank.

Many students spend time learning quotations by heart. This can be useful, but it is important to remember what you are meant to do with quotations once you get into the exam.

By using **The Quotation Bank**, not only will you have a huge number of textual, critical and contextual quotations to use in your essays, you will also have ideas on what to say about them, how to analyse them, how to link them together, and what questions to use them for.

These quotations can form the basis of your answer, making sure every point articulates an informed, personal response **(AO1)** and allows you to analyse ways in which meanings are shaped **(AO2)**.

The critical and contextual quotations allow you to easily and effectively explore the significance and influence of context **(AO3)**, and provide you with a variety of different readings to explore **(AO5)**.

The textual quotations cover the whole text to allow you to show comprehensive whole text knowledge, and the critical and contextual quotations cover the full range of the text's publication history to help you explore the contexts in which the text was both written and received **(AO3)**.

Act One Scene One:
   CORDELIA (aside): "What shall Cordelia speak? Love, and be silent."

Interpretation: Cordelia understands she cannot match the overblown declarations of love heard from Goneril and Regan, and refuses to pander to Lear's destructive vanity. Instead, she must trust their mutually understood love as father and daughter.

Techniques: Rhetorical Question; Imperative.

Analysis:

- As Cordelia's first utterance in the play, her self-questioning and imperative answer introduce an ethos for her character that values genuine emotion over the rhetoric and sycophancy of Goneril and Regan.
- In Cordelia's view, to "speak love" is to be silent. Love does not require elaborate language.
- Cordelia's aside is also intended to guide audience reaction to Lear's demands and the other sisters' answers. She highlights the shallowness of their flattering speech which is motivated by greed.

Use in essays on… Family; Justice; Gender.

Act One Scene One:

LEAR: "Thy truth then be thy dower."

Interpretation: Lear ironically highlights the difference between the land and wealth he has given to Goneril and Regan, and the "truth" that is left to Cordelia. He intends to punish her for failing to declare her love, but the audience recognises that Cordelia's "truth" is much more precious.

Techniques: Irony; Repetition; Language.

Analysis:

- Lear takes up and twists Cordelia's claim to be "true" or loyal, speaking as if loyalty is insufficient for him, but ironically allowing the audience to see that Cordelia is speaking the "truth".
- The repetition of "thy" gives Cordelia ownership of her "truth" – although Lear dismisses the abstract idea as worthless, it is ironically more than he ends with.
- Lear's words address the insecurity that Cordelia faces as a young woman without a "dower" to attract a husband, but her truthfulness is what ultimately persuades the King of France to take her without an inheritance.

Use in essays on... Social Hierarchy; Gender; Family.

Act One Scene Two:

EDMUND: "Why bastard? Wherefore base?"

Interpretation: Edmund complains that due to his illegitimate birth – a thing beyond his control – he is doomed to be seen as inferior and unworthy by others, whatever his personal qualities.

Techniques: Rhetorical Question; Alliteration.

Analysis:

- Shakespeare complicates the audience's reaction to Edmund. He is a key antagonist in the play, and yet his opening argument and rhetorical questions are sympathetic, and the angry, alliterative "b" also conveys a tone of genuine hurt.
- Families with absent mothers appear frequently in Shakespeare's plays. Lear's and Gloucester's families are both fractured and unstable. Gloucester's 'good' son, Edgar, stands to inherit, and his bastard turns against them in the pursuit of land and status.
- Lear, conversely, disinherits the 'good' child, Cordelia, who remains patient and virtuous, whereas Goneril and Regan abuse their inheritance. In both cases the proper transfer from one generation to the next fails.

Use in essays on… Social Hierarchy; Family; Fortune; Identity.

Act One Scene Four:
>   FOOL: "I am better than thou art now. I am a fool, thou art nothing."

Interpretation: Lear has lost his place in the social order, as well as his identity, by abdicating the throne and alienating his family. Without them he is "nothing" and heading for oblivion.

Techniques: Juxtaposition; Metaphor; Repetition.

Analysis:

- The Fool's second phrase bathetically undercuts his first: instead of setting up a joke, he describes Lear's situation with painful directness.
- He repeats one of the play's key motifs, "nothing", to reveal the desperate truth of a King without power or status.
- The Fool's brief declarative statements and use of parallelism in the second sentence suggest self-possession and clarity on his part, in stark contrast to Lear's own uncertainty and rashness. This self-possession is reinforced by the confident repetition of "I am"; even as a lowly "fool", he is able to articulate his own identity and place in the social order.

Use in essays on... Social Hierarchy; Foolishness and Madness; Identity.

Act One Scene Five:

LEAR: "O, let me not be mad."

Interpretation: As Act One comes to an end Lear, perhaps prompted by the Fool's mocking or by reflecting on how he has sabotaged his own happiness, begins to fear madness, and foreshadows his own descent into madness later on.

Techniques: Foreshadowing; Tone.

Analysis:

- The actor and the audience must decide whether Lear is already "mad" in Act One. Was renouncing the throne an act of madness, or his spiteful treatment of Cordelia and Kent? And can Lear already recognise his own madness?
- This part of the play exemplifies Shakespeare's ability to bring psychological reality to his characters. The premise of *King Lear* is almost like a fairy tale, set in the distant past; but the portrayal of an ostracised old man, in fear for the loss of his mind, remains heartbreakingly true to real life.
- The exclamation of "O" creates a tone of pleading and desperation – he already senses that he is losing control of his mind.

Use in essays on… Foolishness and Madness; Identity.

Act Two Scene Two:
> **KENT:** "Nothing almost sees miracles but misery."

Interpretation: Kent (in disguise) sits in the stocks as punishment for his abuse of Oswald. He reads a letter from Cordelia, which offers him hope even in a moment of pain and humiliation.

Techniques: Foreshadowing; Motif.

Analysis:

- Typically of Shakespeare, a seemingly throwaway line by a minor character encapsulates one of the play's central themes: the virtue of suffering. It's only through experiencing "misery" that we can see and appreciate "miracles".

- Kent uses a key motif, "nothing", reflecting how he, like Lear and Edgar elsewhere in the play, lives outside the social order of the court and are vulnerable to suffering.

- The partial phrase "Nothing almost sees miracles" could foreshadow the motif of blindness which is so important later on; indeed, to "peruse this letter" Kent calls for the "warm sun" to be a "beacon" and cast "comfortable beams" so he can read of Cordelia's "remedies".

Use in essays on... Suffering and Redemption; Sight and Blindness.

Act Two Scene Four:
> **REGAN:** "I pray you, father, being weak, seem so."

Interpretation: Regan pressures Lear into giving up his train of knights, asserting her own higher status and position of power. She tries to tell Lear he should forget his followers and live in a way befitting his old age and powerlessness.

Techniques: Imperative; Tone.

Analysis:

- Regan's show of politeness ("I pray you, father") barely disguises her ruthless treatment of Lear. Along with her sister, she calmly negotiates away Lear's entourage of knights, manoeuvring him into irrelevance.
- Lear reacts with contempt to Regan's suggestion, but she has done no more than highlight the truth of Lear's situation. His delusional pride, which caused him to ostracise Cordelia, was what brought about his "weak" state.
- As well as the imperative "seem so", Regan and Goneril hold hands at this moment, visually displaying their united front against Lear.

Use in essays on… Family; Gender; Social Hierarchy.

Act Two Scene Four:
> LEAR: "I abjure all roofs, and choose
> To wage against the enmity o' the air."

Interpretation: Instead of lowering himself within society by agreeing to Regan and Goneril's terms, Lear threatens to leave it altogether. His lines echo those of Edgar, who chooses to "out-face / The winds and persecutions of the sky." Both characters are escaping the (perceived or actual) treachery of their families.

Techniques: Personification; Language.

Analysis:

- Outside of courtly society and the safety of home, the open "air" represents total exposure to the natural world, to fate (the stars are alluded to in references to the sky), and to the pre-Christian gods of King Lear's world.
- For Lear, this escape is an abdication of his place in society but also a form of transcendence. His life nears its end; his kingly power is spent; now he moves beyond the structures of mortal power to subject himself to nature.
- Whilst Lear tries to stress his agency through his ability to "choose", and war-like connotations of "wage", he is left fighting nothing but insubstantial "air".

Use in essays on… Social Hierarchy; Power of Nature.

Act Two Scene Four:
>   LEAR: "Thou art my flesh, my blood, my daughter;
>   Or rather a disease that's in my flesh;
>   Which I must needs call mine."

Interpretation: Lear veers between extreme, conflicting emotions: the idealised image he once held of Goneril and Regan as loving daughters, and the savage contempt he feels when they refuse to accommodate the entourage of knights he considers his due.

Techniques: Repetition; Metaphor.

Analysis:

- The repetition of "my" and "mine" reflect both Lear's sense of betrayal and his self-recrimination at having created his daughters and empowered them against his kingdom.
- Recognition is a central motif in the play; characters both acknowledge and refute the obligations of family and status, while others move in disguise to avoid recognition, and some lose their faculties of sight or clear thought.
- The repetition of "flesh" emphasises the depth of their betrayal – they are a "disease" that has infected Lear, penetrated deep into "my flesh, my blood".

Use in essays on… Family; Gender; Social Hierarchy; Sight and Blindness.

Act Two Scene Four:

> LEAR: "Touch me with noble anger,
> And let not women's weapons, water-drops,
> Stain my man's cheeks!"

Interpretation: As he rages at Regan and Goneril, Lear's language, as it often does, turns to misogyny. He prays to the "heavens" to grant him manly anger befitting his situation.

Techniques: Metaphor; Alliteration; Language.

Analysis:

- The audience learns little about Lear's past in the play, but his attachment to his retinue of knights aligns him with an ideal of masculinity expressed through battle and aggression, reinforced by the chivalric connotations of "noble anger".
- Lear calls tears "women's weapons", but Goneril and Regan are composed and united in this scene. It is Lear whose emotions are changeable and overwhelming. "Water-drops" implies Lear sees women as weak and insubstantial, yet Goneril and Regan are anything but.
- The awkward, alliterative repetition of "w" undercuts Lear's anger; he seems stuttering in the face of his daughters' "weapons".

Use in essays on… Gender; Family.

Act Three Scene One:
> GENTLEMAN: "Contending with the fretful elements;
> Bids the wind blow the earth into the sea."

Interpretation: Here we receive a report of Lear's behaviour. Lear has left his daughters and is roaming the countryside in a storm; the Gentleman's words contrast the vast power of nature with the much smaller domain of human agency.

Techniques: Imagery; Irony; Personification.

Analysis:

- The Gentleman's description of Lear's actions is ironic: in trying to command or "contend with" the elements, Lear instead highlights the limits of his own power.
- The personification of "fretful" suggests rough weather, but also reflects Lear's own angry and agitated state, carried over from his interactions with Goneril and Regan.
- It's significant that Shakespeare offers us this description *before* Lear appears on-stage in the storm. The effect is to undermine Lear: when he arrives we are primed to see him as a pathetic figure, not a god-like one.

Use in essays on… Power of Nature; Social Hierarchy; Foolishness and Madness.

Act Three Scene Two:
> LEAR: "Rumble thy bellyful! Spit, fire! Spout, rain!
> Nor rain, wind, thunder, fire, are my daughters."

Interpretation: As he wanders the heath in foul weather, Lear subjects himself to the mercy of nature, seeing in the power of the storm a kind of natural justice. Here he contrasts that justice with what he calls the "unkindness" of his daughters.

Techniques: Imagery; Personification.

Analysis:
- Lear personifies the weather using bodily imagery ("bellyful" and "spit"), seeming to see nature as a conscious force, as if appealing to a higher authority than those in the human realm. Where else can a king go to contest his power?
- Imagery of "fire" and "rain" suggests Lear is urging on an apocalypse, as a punishment for what he sees as the wickedness of the world, and perhaps for his own actions.
- The list of "rain, wind, thunder, fire," becomes more intense and destructive with each element, but no natural entity matches the ferocity and violence of "my daughters".

Use in essays on… Power of Nature; Gender.

Act Three Scene Three:
> EDMUND: "The younger rises when the old doth fall."

Interpretation: Having displaced Edgar, Edmund is positioning himself to win the inheritance of Gloucester's lands and title by betraying his father to Regan and Cornwall.

Techniques: Antithesis; Irony; Foreshadowing.

Analysis:

- Edmund's words are ironic, in that they betray his evil intentions while reinforcing a commonplace idea reflecting the natural order of things: the old *should* "fall", and the young should rise in their place.
- "Fall" here has two meanings: both the death of the older generation, and the "fall" of Gloucester that Edmund is perpetrating.
- Edmund's antithetical statement ironically foreshadows the play's tragedy: the transfer from the older to younger generations is unnaturally incomplete as Lear's daughters predecease him.
- In Act One Edmund states "Edmund the base shall top the legitimate. I grow". As well as "rises", both "top" and "grow" stress his obsession with social elevation.

Use in essays on... Family; Fortune; Social Hierarchy.

Act Three Scene Four:

> **LEAR:** "Take physic, pomp;
> Expose thyself to feel what wretches feel."

Interpretation: As he finds shelter from the storm, a soaked and filthy Lear imagines poor "wretches" at the margins of society who live without shelter or security. He scorns his own "pomp" (grandness) and reflects on the fact that the storm can teach him compassion for those below him.

Techniques: Imagery; Personification.

Analysis:

- This moment marks a climax in this part of Lear's story. He has renounced the throne, been rejected by his daughters, and suffered the purgation of the storm. Now we glimpse a new, compassionate, humble side to Lear. He evolves again in the next action in the play, with his encounter with Edgar and the mock trial marking the onset (or advancement) of his madness.

- This moment contributes to the play's portrayal of the virtue of suffering and endurance – when he does "expose thyself to feel" the result is a healing one ("physic"), much like Kent in the stocks, where "misery" leads to "remedies".

Use in essays on… Social Hierarchy; Suffering and Redemption; Power of Nature.

Act Three Scene Seven:
>   REGAN: "One side will mock the other – th'other too."

Interpretation: After Cornwall gouges out one of Gloucester's eyes as punishment for delivering Lear to the safety of Dover, Regan, swept up in the thrill of violence, urges him to take the other.

Techniques: Tone; Language.

Analysis:

- Regan's enthusiasm for the torture of Gloucester depicts a savagery in her nature that has previously been concealed by her composure when dealing with political matters.
- The joking tone here, suggesting Gloucester's face needs to be 'evened up' by the removal of the other eye, conveys her sadistic enjoyment. "Mock" also alludes to the lack of respect Regan displays towards Gloucester (and Lear).
- Regan's violence towards Gloucester can easily be read as displaced violence towards her father, Lear. Gloucester's blinding dramatizes his blindness towards the true nature of Edmund, just as Lear misjudged his own children.

Use in essays on… Suffering and Redemption; Justice; Sight and Blindness.

Act Four Scene One:
> EDGAR: "The lowest and most dejected thing of fortune
> Stands still in esperance, lives not in fear."

Interpretation: Edgar, as Poor Tom, reflects that even at the "lowest" there is always hope ("esperance") that things will improve. His words reflect the contemporary idea of the Wheel of Fortune: that the great could always be brought low, and the low raised up.

Techniques: Aphorism; Language.

Analysis:
- These words at the beginning of Act Four introduce the idea of hope into the play. Edgar's discussion of what it is to be the "worst" gives way to a seeming change in "fortune" as Gloucester, then Lear, are reunited with their children.
- Edgar's description of himself as a "thing of fortune" applies equally to Lear and Gloucester: those characters who have left the social order of the Court and political relevance are now subject to the whims of "fortune". The reunion of Edgar and Gloucester, for example, seems almost a coincidence.
- "Thing" emphasises the inconsequential nature of man, whilst "stands still" depicts the passive nature of humanity in the face of "fortune".

Use in essays on… Suffering and Redemption; Fortune; Identity.

Act Four Scene Two:

ALBANY: "O Goneril,
You are not worth the dust which the rude wind
Blows in your face."

Interpretation: Albany excoriates Goneril for her treatment of Lear and the conflict it has sparked.

Techniques: Imagery; Motif.

Analysis:

- As Albany turns against Goneril, the play seems to be moving towards a restoration of justice and order, with its antagonists revealed and Cordelia soon to arrive.
- Albany's words highlight the difference between Goneril's great material "worth" as ruler of half the kingdom, and her "worth" as a person.
- "Rude wind" continues the play's use of hostile weather as a symbol of natural justice. Albany seems to suggest Goneril will be brought to justice.
- The image of "dust" in Goneril's face links to the motif of blindness, a symbol of her poor judgement and lack of morality.

Use in essays on… Justice; Power of Nature; Sight and Blindness.

Act Four Scene Three:
> **CORDELIA:** "No blown ambition doth our arms incite,
> But love, dear love, and our aged father's right."

Interpretation: Cordelia, now Queen of France, is prepared to go to war in Britain, but she remains a figure of virtue in the play, motivated only by "love" and loyalty.

Techniques: Repetition; Antithesis.

Analysis:

- The play keeps its political conflict in the background – the build-up to war is depicted mostly through letters and second-hand reports – but the audience can easily read Goneril and Regan as cruel, tyrannical leaders and Britain as a state in peril.
- Cordelia here reminds us of the virtuous stand she took at the play's beginning, valuing honest "love" over ambitious political game-playing.
- In Cordelia's antithetical statement, "blown (overblown) ambition" is what motivates Goneril and Regan; "dear love" is Cordelia's main motivation, alongside the honourable cause of the restoration of "our aged father's right".

Use in essays on… Justice; Social Hierarchy; Gender; Identity.

Act Four Scene Five:
> EDGAR: "Thy life's a miracle. Speak yet again."

Interpretation: Edgar tricks his blind father Gloucester into believing the gods have intervened to save his life. He rescues Gloucester – the character who has arguably suffered most – from despair by convincing him of the essential value of his life.

Techniques: Language; Motif.

Analysis:

- The reunions of Act Four – Edgar with Gloucester and Cordelia with Lear – bring humanity and compassion into the play. Here, even the life of a blind old man on the verge of suicide is precious ("a miracle") and worth saving.
- "Speak yet again" echoes Lear's instruction to Cordelia to "Speak again" in Act One. The situation is reversed: instead of a father demanding flattery from a child, now a child is rejoicing in their father, and by asking that Gloucester "speak yet again", is subtly restoring a sense of agency to his father.
- Once again related to what Kent articulates in Act One, it is "misery" that allows us to see "miracles".

Use in essays on… Suffering and Redemption; Family.

Act Four Scene Five:
> LEAR: "Through tatter'd clothes great vices do appear;
> Robes and furr'd gowns hide all."

Interpretation: The "mad" Lear, rambling on the perceived injustice of the world, makes this observation on how people of high status are protected from facing justice for their crimes.

Techniques: Metonymy; Irony.

Analysis:

- "Tatter'd clothes" are a metonym for poverty and lowliness; "Robes and furr'd gowns" for wealth and high status.
- Lear, Gloucester and Edgar are the characters who have lost their high status; they are the ones persecuted and hunted by Goneril and Regan.
- Lear could also be referring to his own time as King: when he wore "robes", his own faults were concealed or unacknowledged. Once he lost that status, he became a victim.
- "Do appear" implies poverty and lowliness are not the cause of "vices"; "vices" are ever-present throughout society, but the upper strata are able to "hide all".

Use in essays on... Justice; Social Hierarchy; Sight and Blindness.

Act Five Scene Two:

EDGAR: "Men must endure
Their going hence even as their coming hither.
Ripeness is all."

Interpretation: Death ("going hence") is inevitable; its certainty must be endured as a part of life, just as the pains of life must be endured from birth ("coming hither").

Techniques: Aphorism; Metaphor; Tone.

Analysis:

- By "Ripeness", Edgar appears to mean that men must be ready to endure what trials life may bring, and to face their end when it comes.
- The metaphor of a fruit that is "ripe" implies it is at its best and fullest, but also at the point of a kind of death by detaching from its plant.
- Edgar's role in the play links to the restoration of order, but his moralising, even lecturing tone alongside his aphoristic language can seem jarring, and increasingly detached from the tragedy and grief towards which the play is heading.

Use in essays on… Suffering and Redemption; Justice; Identity.

Act Five Scene Three:
> EDGAR: "His flawed heart,
> Alack, too weak the conflict to support,
> 'Twixt two extremes of passion, joy and grief,
> Burst smilingly."

Interpretation: Gloucester died, according to Edgar, overwhelmed by the conflicting "joy" of Edgar revealing his identity, and "grief" at his own past actions and suffering.

Techniques: Antithesis; Juxtaposition.

Analysis:

- The juxtaposition of "Burst smilingly" could indicate that Edgar is romanticising his father's death, giving the audience an account that matches his own moralistic ideas and idealised relationship with Gloucester.
- Edgar's account suggests "extremes" of "joy and grief" can be reconciled in a happy death, but the play undercuts this message with the deaths of Cordelia and Lear.
- "Flawed heart" is a literal reference to the heart attack that killed him, but also symbolises Gloucester's emotional "flawed heart" that caused "the conflict" between him and his sons.

Use in essays on... Suffering and Redemption.

Act Five Scene Three:
> EDMUND: "I was contracted to them both; all three
> Now marry in an instant."

Interpretation: Edmund's manipulation of Goneril and Regan ("contracted to them both"), and their jostling for power, comes to nothing. He and the two women will soon join ("marry"), but only in death. The scheming of the play's antagonists is over.

Techniques: Tone; Irony; Foreshadowing.

Analysis:
- Edmund's bitter, joking remark encapsulates the superficiality of Goneril and Regan in contrast to the deeper emotional journey taken by Lear, Gloucester and Edgar.
- Ambition and manipulation destroyed the sisters, but other characters found meaning and fulfilment outside of the political world.
- Reference to "all three" remind the audience of the third daughter, Cordelia, whose life hangs in the balance, and foreshadows the loss of Lear's youngest child.

Use in essays on… Social Hierarchy; Gender; Justice.

Act Five Scene Three:
> KENT: "If Fortune brag of two she loved and hated,
> One of them we behold."

Interpretation: Kent sees the anguished Lear and the dead Cordelia, whom Edgar and Albany tried to save but moments too late, as exemplifying the changeability of "Fortune".

Techniques: Antithesis; Personification.

Analysis:

- Kent's words summarise the role "Fortune" has played in *King Lear*, and how the play dramatizes Fortune's "wheel" as characters are raised and brought low through poor judgement, extraneous circumstances and coincidence.
- The tension between "Fortune" and human agency is a central theme in Shakespeare's plays. Was it "Fortune", mere coincidence, or the actions of Edmund or Lear himself which ultimately caused Cordelia's death?
- Kent's ambiguous antithesis of "loved and hated" asks the question of whether "Fortune" smiled on Lear and Cordelia by reuniting them before death. "Brag" certainly implies "Fortune" is not an entirely benevolent force.

Use in essays on… Fortune; Suffering and Redemption.

Act Five Scene Three:
> KENT: "The wonder is he hath endured so long;
> He but usurped his life."

Interpretation: Kent makes sense of Lear's death, paying tribute to the spirit of an old and frail man who "endured" great suffering.

Techniques: Metaphor; Language.

Analysis:

- Kent calls Lear's endurance a "wonder": Lear was strong indeed to live so long, and this echoes the play's idea of the virtue of endurance.
- Lear's carrying of Cordelia's body, in this context, can be seen as a visual symbol of his strength at the end, and the redemption found in his reunion with Cordelia.
- "Usurped his life" suggests Lear's inner vitality was strong enough to push through his failing health, not letting it defeat him. As a former King, however, Lear can be said to have "usurped" himself at the beginning of the story by renouncing power, setting events into motion.

Use in essays on… Suffering and Redemption; Fortune.

Nahum Tate (1681) describes how,

"This method necessarily threw me on making the Tale conclude in a success to the innocent distressed persons: Otherwise I must have encumbered the stage with dead bodies."

Interpretation: Tate's adapted version of *King Lear* appeared in 1681 and was the best-known and most-performed version of the play until 1838. Tate made significant changes, for example a new 'happy' ending in which Lear regains the throne and Cordelia marries Edgar.

Analysis:

- To 17th and 18th century audiences, including influential thinkers such as Samuel Johnson, the virtues of *King Lear* were marred by an ending which did not reflect "natural ideas of justice".

- The procession of "dead bodies" at the end – the text calls for the bodies of all three of Lear's daughters to be on stage, although some directors avoid this – might seem essential to modern audiences, but Tate worked in a time when Shakespeare was seen as a genius, but not an untouchable one. Re-writing the play to reflect the audience's sense of "justice" was seen as an improvement.

Use in essays on… Structure and Stagecraft; Fortune.

William Hazlitt (1817) claimed,

"The mind of Lear […] is like a tall ship driven about by the winds, buffeted by the furious waves, but that still rides above the storm, having its anchor fixed in the bottom of the sea […] or like the solid promontory pushed from its basis by the force of an earthquake."

Interpretation: Hazlitt sees in *King Lear* the Romantic aesthetic of the Sublime. "Sublime" describes a type of beauty found in the awe we feel at the vastness and power of nature.

Analysis:

- Hazlitt writes that the power of *King Lear* comes from the supposedly unbreakable bond of "filial piety" – duty between parent and child – being broken, and the "giddy anarchy and whirling tumult" that results.
- In Hazlitt's reading, the storm on the heath becomes the image of the power of natural bonds breaking. Lear's mental anguish is itself a "sublime" phenomenon, as vast and overwhelming as a "storm" or "earthquake".
- In the first simile Lear is "driven" and "buffeted" but remains with his "anchor fixed"; in the second "the solid promontory [is] pushed from its basis." Which is the more appropriate depiction of "the mind of Lear"?

Use in essays on… Foolishness and Madness; Power of Nature.

John Keats (1818) described *King Lear* as,
> "The fierce dispute / Betwixt damnation and impassion'd clay."

Interpretation: The Romantic poet Keats revered Shakespeare, and *King Lear* in particular. This quotation is from a sonnet: *On Sitting Down to Read King Lear Once Again*. His suggestive description of the play implies a conflict between punishment and suffering on one hand, and the strength of human emotions on the other.

Analysis:

- "Clay" as a Biblical symbol represents how people are shaped by God, but also their fragility. There is a suggestive link with the discussion in *King Lear* of what forces shape the people we are.
- "Impassion'd clay" suggests the play depicts humans in both their basest bodily form ("clay") and at their most emotional and irrational ("impassion'd").
- Keats coined the term "negative capability": the ability of artists such as Shakespeare to let uncertainty and doubt ("the fierce dispute") guide their work, instead of pursuing a particular philosophical truth. How would you apply this to *King Lear*?

Use in essays on... Suffering and Redemption; Identity.

A.C. Bradley (1904) stated,
> "*King Lear* seems to me Shakespeare's greatest achievement,
> but it seems to me not his best play."

Interpretation: Bradley draws a distinction between the effectiveness of certain moments and ideas in *King Lear*, and its lack of coherence as a whole.

Analysis:
- Bradley illuminates the difference between studying *King Lear* (or any play) on the page and seeing it performed. The blinding of Gloucester, for example, can be given symbolic or thematic significance in reading; on stage it is a "blot", its violence overpowering any meaning.
- Bradley explains some points of contention in the play as deliberate; others as inconsistencies that (in his view) Shakespeare chose to ignore to preserve the dramatic effect of particular moments. Could Gloucester really believe Edmund's letter plot? Why does the Fool disappear without explanation? Why does Edgar not reveal himself to Gloucester earlier, and why was that moment kept offstage? These questions arise when we analyse the play; they may not be significant to its effect or meaning in the theatre.

Use in essays on... Structure and Stagecraft; Suffering and Redemption.

Kathleen McLuskie (1985) argues that,

"Cordelia's saving love, so much admired by critics, works in the action less as a redemption for womankind than as an example of patriarchy restored."

Interpretation: Cordelia is seen in the play's opening as virtuous, but while her rebellion against Lear is very different from that of Goneril and Regan, it is a rebellion nonetheless. Her reappearance at the end is only heroic in that it re-affirms the bond of duty and love she owes Lear.

Analysis:

- McLuskie writes that *King Lear* insists on "the connection between evil women and a chaotic world."

- Although modern audiences might see the play as one in which women have agency, and Cordelia can even be viewed heroically, in McLuskie's reading this is always set against an ideal of duty to the "patriarchy", which the play makes sure is "restored".

- Lear's anger at his daughters expresses itself through bitterly misogynistic, dehumanising imagery, as in the "centaur" speech in Act 4. How far is Cordelia's love for her father undermined by his view of women?

Use in essays on... Gender; Social Hierarchy; Identity.

R. A. Foakes (1997) suggests,

"Its exposure of the horror of torture and suffering no longer seems outrageous in the context of concentration camps, napalm bombs, anti-personnel mines, and acts of terrorism."

Interpretation: Foakes summarises the changing attitude to *King Lear* since the Second World War. It is often seen now as Shakespeare's greatest work and intensely contemporary, aligning with what we know about violence, justice and human nature today, rather than how they were idealised in the past.

Analysis:

- In the 18th and 19th centuries, Western Europe promoted ideals of human progress and the spread of civilisation. Of course, this idea was often a fig leaf for violence and racism. The "torture and suffering" of two World Wars destroyed these moral certainties.
- *King Lear* portrays a world in which humans are reduced to their basest, most vulnerable state and obey their worst, cruellest instincts. When Albany tells Edgar and Kent at the end to "sustain" the "gored state", there is no sense of healing or progress for the Britain that will follow.

Use in essays on… Suffering and Redemption; Justice.

Fintan O'Toole (2002) wrote,
"Lear, far from being a man from the mists of time, is not even a feudal lord – he is an archetype of the new middle-class man."

Interpretation: O'Toole challenges the view of *King Lear* as inhabiting a "fairy-tale" or "pre-Christian" milieu, and restores it to the contemporary world of Jacobean England, in which old certainties about societal order were giving way to the modern world of capitalism.

Analysis:
- O'Toole asserts that Lear has no status once he gives his land away – he "is not even a feudal lord", let alone a powerful King. His power was based on his worth, not on a conception of a divinely-appointed King at the head of the social order.
- O'Toole extends this idea to Edmund's character: "His is the world of the self-made man, in which we have no-one else to blame for our sins, and no-one else to thank for our good fortune." The play openly contrasts this view with Kent's belief in astrological influence, and Gloucester's ordering of Edgar and Edmund according to their birth.

Use in essays on… Social Hierarchy; Fortune; Identity.

Ian McKellen (2008) said,

"He goes on a tortuous and terrifying emotional journey, but by the end he has achieved some reconciliation to his own position in the real world, and that includes love for family and respect and regard for friends."

Interpretation: McKellen, one of the most respected Shakespearean actors of the 20th and 21st century, gives his account of Lear's journey through the play. He links Lear's "reconciliation [with] the real world" to his diminishing reliance on the gods.

Analysis:

- If Lear reaches a better understanding of his humanity in the play, is it really a tragedy? According to McKellen, "these labels don't mean much".
- Does McKellen's account seem like a simplification, or even naïve about the truths revealed by the play?
- His words speak to the age-old problem of the play's meaning and coherence. This is a work which was once felt to be unfit to perform in Shakespeare's own version, and later as entirely fitting because it speaks to the worst horrors of modern society. But it always remains a *play*, designed for performance, challenging actors and directors to produce a coherent vision.

Use in essays on… Structure and Stagecraft; Suffering and Redemption.

James Shapiro (2015) asserts that,

> "From its opening scene, when a map of Britain is brought on stage, *King Lear* wrestles with what Britishness means, especially in relationship to the longstanding national identities it superseded."

Interpretation: Audiences in 1606 would have drawn parallels between Lear's division of his kingdom and James I's public desire to unite England and Scotland. What is gained, and risked, in the splitting and joining of kingdoms?

Analysis:

- Lear's Britain is an ambiguous, liminal space, caught between the regionalism of Regan and Goneril's separate domains, and the directionless wandering of Lear and Gloucester. It is a hostile, polarised country, with rulers in their castles, and Lear's "poor naked wretches" exposed to the elements.
- Only at Dover does a type of beauty, or at least normality, emerge as Edgar describes the sights from the cliff: "the fishermen that walk upon the beach / appear like mice".
- When Cordelia arrives as Queen of France, does the audience interpret this as a foreign conquest, or welcome home a cheated British queen?

Use in essays on... Social Hierarchy; Identity.

Adam Gopnik (2016) argues,

"He was perfectly aware that the social order he saw before him was arbitrary and unjust, but he was convinced that its absence would lead to chaos and cruelty, not to liberation and kindness."

Interpretation: Gopnik explains how Shakespeare's sensibility was different to our own. He asserted the value of social order even when that order was flawed ("arbitrary and unjust"). In his tragedies, death awaits those who transgress that order: think of *Romeo and Juliet* or *Othello*.

Analysis:

- We know little about Lear's kingdom before his decision to divide it between his daughters, and there is evidence Lear is a manipulative, egotistical ruler. But his absence at the head of the "social order" leaves a void that Goneril, Regan and their husbands fill with power struggles and "chaos and cruelty".
- Outside of the "social order", Lear and Gloucester experience a type of redemption, but only through great suffering. It cannot be called "liberation". Lear's death might have restored "order" had Cordelia lived to take the throne, but the story very deliberately does not allow this.

Use in essays on… Social Hierarchy; Suffering and Redemption; Justice.

Performance History

During Shakespeare's lifetime, *King Lear* was certainly less popular than *Hamlet*, *Othello* or *Macbeth*. From 1681 to 1838 Nahum Tate's *The History of King Lear*, a significant re-writing of Shakespeare's work, delighted audiences: Cordelia survives as Queen with Edgar as King; the Fool is absent; and Lear and Gloucester survive. Restoration audiences revelled in Tate's focus on monarchical order and legitimacy, as well as a 'happy' ending, and it was the British, not the French, who restore the throne.

The prominence given to the war between France and Britain can influence interpretation. How obvious are the political and military consequences of Lear's choices? Whilst modern audiences often engage in the play's personal tragedies, wider political concerns can be of great interest. In Adrian Noble's 1993 RSC production a map of Lear's kingdom covers the stage floor; as the kingdom disintegrates and pulls apart, so too does the map, perhaps representing Lear's greatest crime as King – not the disintegration of his family unit, but of a kingdom he tears apart.

Lear's personal choices as the catalyst for the play's action can be a key focus. In Trevor Nunn's 2007 production the war plot is still evident through elaborate military costume, but there is also an emphasis on the multi-faceted nature of Lear as an individual; a kind, loving father, yet abusive and cruel leader. Perhaps most famously, McKellen's Lear is a vulnerable, fragile old man, encapsulated by his nudity on stage during exile, a visual representation of the fundamental humanity at the heart of the play.

Yet it is also a deeply spiritual play, be it Christian or Pagan, and the role of fate, fortune and the gods as central to the play's tragedy is regularly foregrounded – settings of Stonehenge-style landscapes and ancient runes are often utilised to emphasise the futility of human action against the backdrop of gods who "kill us for their sport". Antony Sher's Lear in Gregory Doran's 2016 production employs pagan imagery, ritualistic behaviours and a giant copper sun as symbols of a life beyond human control, driven by a natural (or indeed supernatural) force beyond human comprehension.

How to revise effectively.

One mistake people often make is to try to revise EVERYTHING!

This is clearly not possible.

Instead, once you understand the text in detail, a good idea is to pick five or six major themes, and four or five major characters, and revise these in great detail. The same is true when exploring key scenes – you are unlikely to be able to closely analyse every single line, so focus on the *skills* of analysis and interpretation and then be ready for any question, rather than covering the whole text and trying to pre-prepare everything.

If, for example, you revised Cordelia and Suffering and Redemption, you will also have covered a huge amount of material to use in questions about Family, Gender or Goneril and Regan.

It is also sensible to avoid revising quotations in isolation; instead, bring together two or three textual quotations as well as a critical and contextual quotation so that any argument you make is supported and explored in detail.

Finally, make sure material is pertinent to the questions you will be set. By revising the skills of interpretation and analysis you will be able to answer the actual question set in the exam, rather than the one you wanted to come up.

Suggested Revision Activities

A great cover and repeat exercise – Cover the whole page, apart from the quotation at the top. Can you now fill in the four sections without looking – Interpretations, Techniques, Analysis, Use in essays on…?

This also works really well as **a revision activity with a friend** – cover the whole page, apart from the quotation at the top. If you read out the quotation, can they tell you the four sections without looking – Interpretations, Techniques, Analysis, Use in essays on…?

For both activities, could you extend the analysis and interpretation further, or provide an alternative interpretation? Also, can you find another quotation that extends or counters the point you have just made?

Your very own Quotation Bank! Using the same headings and format as The Quotation Bank, find 10 more quotations from throughout the text (select them from many different sections of the text to help develop whole text knowledge) and create your own revision cards.

Essay writing – They aren't always fun, but writing essays is great revision. Devise a practice question and try taking three quotations and writing out a perfect paragraph, making sure you add connectives, technical vocabulary and sophisticated language.

Glossary

Alliteration – Repetition of the same consonant or sound at the beginning of a number of words in a sentence: the awkward, alliterative repetition of "w" in "women's weapons" undercuts Lear's anger.

Antithesis – When two opposing ideas are structured together to accentuate the contrast between them: in Cordelia's antithetical statement, "blown ambition" is what motivates Goneril and Regan; "dear love" is Cordelia's main cause.

Aphorism – A concise statement that expresses a general truth: Edgar's role in the play links to the restoration of order, but his moralising tone and aphorisms can seem jarring as he lectures his father.

Foreshadowing – When the writer alludes to or makes reference to something that is yet to come in the text: the partial phrase "nothing almost sees miracles" could foreshadow the motif of blindness which is so important later on.

Imagery – Figurative language that appeals to the senses of the audience: imagery of "fire" and "rain" suggests Lear is urging on an apocalypse, as a punishment for what he sees as the wickedness of the world, and perhaps for his own actions.

Imperative – a sentence that gives a command or an order: as well as the imperative "seem so", Regan and Goneril hold hands at this moment, visually displaying their united front against Lear.

Irony – A statement that suggests one thing but often has a contrary meaning: the Gentleman's description of Lear's actions is ironic – in trying to command or "contend with" the elements, Lear instead highlights the limits of his own power.

Juxtaposition – Two ideas, images or words placed next to each other to create a contrasting effect: the juxtaposition of "burst smilingly" could indicate that Edgar is romanticising his father's death.

Language – The vocabulary chosen to create effect.

Metaphor – A word or phrase used to describe something else so that the first idea takes on the associations of the second: a fruit that is "ripe" implies it is at its best and fullest, but also on the point of a kind of death by detaching from its plant.

Metonymy – A word or phrase where one idea or object is used to signify something it is closely associated with: "tatter'd clothes" are a metonym for poverty and lowliness; "Robes and furr'd gowns" for wealth and high status.

Motif – A significant idea, element or symbol repeated throughout the text: the Fool echoes one of the play's key motifs, "nothing", to reveal the desperate truth of a King without power or status.

Personification – A non-human object or concept takes on human qualities to make its presence more vivid to the audience: Lear personifies the weather using bodily imagery ("bellyful" and "spit"), seeming to see nature as a conscious force.

Repetition – When a word, phrase or idea is repeated to reinforce it: the repetition of "my" and "mine" reflect both Lear's sense of betrayal and his self-recrimination at having created his daughters and empowered them against his kingdom.

Rhetorical Question – A persuasive device where the person asking the question already knows the answer: Shakespeare complicates the audience's reaction to Edmund. He is a key antagonist in the play, and yet his opening argument and rhetorical questions are sympathetic.

Tone – The mood or atmosphere created by the writer: the exclamation of 'O' creates a tone of pleading and desperation – Lear already senses that he is losing control of his mind.

Acknowledgements:

N Tate: *The Epistle Dedicatory* from *The History of King Lear* 1681

S Johnson: *Preface to Shakespeare* 1765

W Hazlitt: *Characters of Shakespeare's Plays* 1817

J Keats: *On Sitting Down to Read King Lear Once Again* 1818

A.C. Bradley: *Shakespearean Tragedy – Lectures on Hamlet, Othello, King Lear, Macbeth*, published by MacMillan and Co 1904

K McLuskie: *The Patriarchal Bard* from *Political Shakespeare: Essays in Cultural Materialism*, edited by J Dollimore and A Sinfield, published by Cornell University Press 1985

R A Foakes: *Introduction to King Lear* from *King Lear*, published by The Arden Shakespeare 1997

F O'Toole: *Shakespeare is Hard, But So is Life: A Radical Guide to Shakespearian Tragedy,* published by Granta 2002

I McKellen: Interview from *King Lear* DVD, directed by T Nunn and C Hunt, Royal Shakespeare Company and The Performance Company 2007

J Shapiro: *1606: William Shakespeare and the Year of Lear*, published by Faber and Faber 2015

A Gopnik: *Why Rewrite Shakespeare?*, published by *The New Yorker* October 2016 Issue